Doors of the Morning

The doors of the morning must open.
The keys of the night are not thrown away.

Carl Sandburg

Doors of the Morning

the winning poems
of the 1996
Sandburg-Livesay Anthology Contest

judged by Fred Cogswell

UnMon America
Pittsburgh, 1997

Poems copyright © the authors, 1997
This collection copyright © Unfinished Monument Press, 1997
Cover illustration copyright © Gilda Mekler, 1997
All rights reserved

Library of Congress Cataloging-in-Publication Data

Doors of the morning : the winning poems of the 1996 Sandburg-Livesay
    Anthology Contest / judged by Fred Cogswell.
        p.   cm.
    ISBN 1-884206-03-4 (paperback)
    1. American poetry—20th century. 2. Canadian poetry—20th century.
 3. Australian poetry—20th century. 4. English poetry—20th century.
 I. Cogswell, Fred, 1917–   . II. Sandburg–Livesay Anthology Contest.
 PS615.D65   1997
 811'.5408—dc21   97-24454
                                                              CIP

The couplet by Carl Sandburg opposite the title page is taken from the poem "Pass, Friend," from the collection *Honey and Salt* (New York: Harcourt, Brace & World, 1963). Reprinted by permission of Harcourt Brace & Company.

UnMon America

(a division of Unfinished Monument Press)
PO Box 4279
Pittsburgh, PA
15203

Unfinished Monument Press is a subsidiary of
Mekler & Deahl, Publishers

Cover illustration: "Moon at Panmure" by Gilda Mekler
Design by Gilda Mekler
Film by SE Graphics
Printing by Transcontinental

Table of Contents

Carol Rose, *pillar of salt* 2
    they talk theology instead 3
Elinor Benedict, *Paper Flowers* 4
    Message to Myself on My Birthday 5
Jim C. Wilson,
    At Edlingham Church, Northumbria, 10th March 1996 10
    The Dark Bird 11
John Souster, *To John Clare* 12
Anne Ashworth, *For Ireland* 13
Winona Baker, *The Wintering Land* 14
David Barnett, *Outback* 15
Paul Berry, *Brandeston School Oak* 17
Mike Boland, *Starlings* 18
Brian Burke, *this old barn* 19
Mavis Carter, *The Place of Wolves* 20
    Windows 21
    Chiselling the Dark 22
    Algarve Spring 23
R.L. Cook, *At Cunninghill* 24
Barbara Crupi, *Flamenco* 25
Marguerite Dolsen, *The Calligrapher* 26
Gerald England, *Clinging to the Valley* 27
Ian Enters, *Aphrodite in Spring* 28
Katherine L. Gordon, *November Storm* 29
David A. Groulx, *Penemue and the Indians* 30
Richard M. Grove, *February Evening Sky* 31
Alistair Halden, *Fulmars* 32
Margaret B. Hammer, *High-Rise Mondrian* 33
F.R. Harris, *We Had Our Targets* 34
David Hillen, *Suddenly* 35
Mary Hodgson, *Saybrook Point, Connecticut* 36
    Peter and the Boys 38
    Elderberry Harvest 39
Peter Howard, *Love Letter to Brigitte Helm* 40
Winifred N. Hulbert, *Manitoba Farmers* 42
Sheila Hyland, *Summer Daze* 44
Laura H. Kennedy, *Leaving Ash Creek* 45
Mary Kratt, *At the Mercury Mill* 46
    Widow 47
    Kinfolk 48
    Factory Whistles, Early 1900s, North Carolina 50
Cecil Justin Lam, *Morning Report* 51

John B. Lee, *The Coal Miners* 52
    The Winter of 96 54
    I Think Continually of Those Who Are Truly Average 55
Anne Lewis-Smith, *Isandlwana* 56
    Widow 57
Noah Leznoff, *the wind is blowing me away* 58
    teacher 59
    In Moonlight After Rain 60
Michael Londry, *What Makes You Feel*
              You Are Suited to This Type of Employment? ... 61
Hugh MacDonald, *The Digging of Deep Wells* 62
    Behind the Red Brick House 64
Tanis MacDonald, *Service with a Smile* 66
Colin Mackay, *Bosnian Elegy* 67
    Bosnian Village 70
John Marks, *Bosnia* 71
Joy Martin, *Night of the Gale* 72
Catherine McCausland, *No Pilot Required* 73
Jane McCreery, *Turnpike World Series* 74
Derrick McIntosh, *Proverb of Poverty* 75
Elise McKay, *No Miracle* 77
    The Ammonite 78
Hilary Mellon, *Marbled Moon* 79
Chad Norman, *Wall Against the Back* 80
Mary Nugent, *Rievaulx Abbey* 81
Margaret Pain, *Dawn Watch* 83
Peggy Poole, *Needlewoman* 84
Barbara Rennie, *Au Moulin de la Galette* 85
Louise Rogers, *Entering Cold Woodlands* 86
K.V. Skene, *Learning Death* 87
Deirdre Armes Smith, *Woman of Inishmaan* 88
    Cottage at High Riley 90
Gwen Stanley, *Dawn Chorus* 91
Andrew Stickland, *A Leaving Present* 92
    Evensong 93
Elizabeth St Jacques, *A Star Shines On* 94
Mildred Tremblay, *Breasts and Bellies* 95
Ruth Waldram, *The Studio at Aix* 97
Janet Walker, *Darkening Walk* 99
Maureen Weldon, *El Alamein* 100
Duane Williams, *Nobody Said Anything* 101
Ray Wilson, *"Good fences make good neighbours"* 103
Margaret Winter, *The Journey Back* 104
Joan Woodcock, *Hands* 105
Richard Woollatt, *Roy Ellergodt* 106

Introduction

by James Deahl

Doors of the Morning, dedicated to the memory of Carl Sandburg and to his lasting contribution to world literature, starts an annual series of anthologies. These volumes will celebrate a special kind of poetry — the kind usually described in America as Populist Poetry and in Canada as People's Poetry.

Populist Poetry became a force upon the publication of Sandburg's *Chicago Poems* in 1916. This was followed in 1918 by *Cornhuskers,* which earned Sandburg the first of three Pulitzer Prizes; yet the critics of the day paid scant attention. A new generation of critics arose in the years after World War II, among them Selden Rodman, who wrote of a "proletarian" poetry characterized by "the idea of democracy — that conviction of the innate worth of every man." Rodman saw a poetry, rooted in Whitman, that was sensual and expressed a great love for mankind. This poetry was frank, realistic, and passionate. Moreover, in the hands of writers like Muriel Rukeyser, it "achieved a fusion of tenderness and indignation." Current practitioners in this tradition include Maggie Anderson and Peter Oresick. Perhaps Walt Whitman's spirit lives within their work.

In Canada, People's Poetry has been a parallel, not a derivative, development. Poets such as Milton Acorn, Dorothy Livesay, and Raymond Souster were less likely to turn to Whitman for inspiration than to Archibald Lampman — a Red Tory with an outlook very different from Whitman's. People's Poetry properly begins with the publication of Livesay's *Day and Night* in 1944. For over fifty years, people's literature has been the mainstream of Canadian literature. Perhaps the spirit of Lampman can be discerned in the poetry of John B. Lee.

Late last year, *Poetry Review* took note of the New Populism sweeping Britain. While it remains to be seen what this will lead to, a fresh movement — complete with its own anthology, *Emergency Kit* — has come onto the scene to promote the idea that poetry can be relevant to the daily lives of ordinary people and can speak to people using common language. This is poetry actually written for people, not for some academic elite, and we need more of it in our lives.

Prize-winning Poem

CAROL ROSE

pillar of salt

you stand resplendent in the sun
an ancient shrine   relic from a cult
like your name   long forgotten
there's mystery in your womanform
cast in crystal or made of tears
when not even ten in His image
could be called worthy   & you were
left shimmering in the sand
witness to a time
when looking back was sacred

they talk theology instead

has your passion ever been met?

an opening that probes past
permitted terrain   opens the soul
exposes the chaos he fears

what i've done is fight   love
my children   write   keeps me
out of the dark zone   the night
sweats   nazis & demons far
from my bed

hardly the answer she imagined
they talk theology instead   angels
dance on the tips of their questions
beings of light   whirling at the edge

Prize-winning Poem

ELINOR BENEDICT

Paper Flowers

*Hall of Revolutionary Martyrs,
Tianjin, China, January 14, 1980*

1

An official hands out paper flowers. We pin them
on our coats, my daughter and I, following
our Chinese cousins into the Hall of Martyrs.
Cold flows from stone; an ocean closes behind us.
Our footsteps speak the only language we know:
Stop. Stop. We shouldn't have come.

2

In the anteroom we sip black tea. We try
to warm our hands on the cups while guests
fill the table like a jury. I bow my head, feeling
my daughter accuse me of mourning a woman I hardly knew.
Dear girl: She was my father's only sister.
You don't know yet, how that is.

3

The bald man beckons. We file into a chamber where
hundreds of gray flowers clutter the walls. From a hood
of black crepe her photograph gazes. I close my eyes.
Last time I saw her, the wind flew her hat like a kite
over the seashells, over the blue umbrella, at my father's
old house. She laughed when he caught it,
my father her brother again.

4

Four times we bow to her ashes now boxed in a vault.
Men in gray suits collect all the flowers, stuff
them in cardboard for the next quick blooming. I'm dry
as the petals they crush, until someone touches my shoulder,
an old woman in black. She takes my daughter's hand,
reaches for mine. She says nothing, but her cheekbones
are wet, her eyes alive with the shock of love.

Message to Myself on My Birthday

June 4, 1989, Tiananmen Square, Beijing

1

This is the day you were born.

Summer in Tennessee, a long time ago,
when people feared dust, debt,
and that drymouth feeling the voice
over the radio's crackle called
fear itself.

In your mother's hot room
you lay naked and yelling.
Your father's sister
came to say goodbye, holding
a baby of her own, half-Chinese,
leaving with a man
who'd changed her country,
her mind.

2

When you were a girl
you learned her story
from snapshots, gifts from abroad,
bits of gossip around the holiday table.
You caught those glances
between your father, your uncles,
their red-faced silence.

Lula the cook served the meal
as if she didn't see.
She took care of you, knew
the family secrets.
You were surprised she had two children
of her own. You saw them
when Mama drove Lula home downtown.
Two small boys darker than their mother
came up and stared at you
through the car window.

Once when you wouldn't behave,
Lula said, *Don't you act
so biggity, Miss Priss. Your aunt
done married a Chinaman.*

3

For years your world
was made of papier mache,
yellow newspapers full of war stories
crumpled in a ball.
You lost your aunt's face
among armies and arguments,
hid her name in the fear
you wanted to forget.

Then one day
a letter rose from the mail
thin as smoke, strangely marked,
a phoenix among sparrows,
announcing she was alive,
coming back to die.

When she arrived
you were astonished she could
laugh. Her stories of concubines
and conquerors, noodles
and murders
brought to your kitchen
the underside of the earth.
Talk made you sisters:
two women remembering
the days they were young.

4

After her memorial
in the cold Hall of Martyrs
your cousins took you to see
the sights of Beijing, a careful
gift for American kin.

You stood among strangers
in Tiananmen Square, winter
all around, your aunt
in ashes.

Quietly, proudly,
your cousins showed you the monument
where the death of Zhou Enlai
brought thousands of paper flowers,
black ink verses
to honor him, to mourn
their loss of more
than voices could say.

5

Today you watch
Tiananmen Square from afar
flickering in a box,
seething in white June heat.
Crowds gather again,
sons and daughters of heroes,
wearing faded jeans, headbands,
cocking their fingers
in the borrowed V. They push
a plaster goddess they hope
will save them.

Their voices cry out those words
you have heard so often
in your own language:
Freedom, Justice.
Lightning nicks the air
smelling like hot metal.

You want to call out
*Wait! Take care. Breathe
deeply.* But they are born
in front of you, slim legs walking
toward the growling
column of tanks.

Then that one small man
dares the machine to crush him.
A cry begins,
the same cry you heard
in another stone place
filled with faces of all colors,
bearing the eyes of brothers,
sisters —

Listen — the air still vibrates
with the voice of that man
whose dark face shone
in the downcast gaze of
Lincoln in his chair
the voice of a servant
dreaming the end
of suffering

Free at last, free at last!

The students of Beijing
strain to hear him.
Thunder rolls,
rain clatters, the earth
shakes as if it is opening.
Naked and yelling

we are born.

Honourable Mention

JIM C. WILSON

At Edlingham Church, Northumbria, 10th March 1996

At one of Christianity's cradles, mist
is thinning on the moors. Our early walk
is to the castle's broken walls, but first
we pass the church, a low grey place of rock.
And with the singing of the wind, a psalm
blends in with high birds calling. Words of praise
have risen here since Bede, exalting Rome,
grew blind while writing histories. March clouds
prohibit the sun. Chilled, we stand as still
as gravestones. The castle's tower leans, held
only by a new steel strut. Then voices tell
us worship's over. Folk file out; some nod.
A congregation numbering only five,
warmed by calor gas, keeping God alive.

The Dark Bird

He's stiller than the reeds and trees.
We wonder if he's even there at all
until, after forever, a gaunt sculpture
skirts the lake-edge on unearthly legs.

Leaves rot and scum the moss-green water
but his black gaze is needling through the murk.
His head unleashed goes stabbing into silver.
Then swiftest swallowing, repositioning.

At night the dark bird's out there waiting.
Sometimes he soars like death and shrieks so loud
the garden echoes, becomes an ancient swampland.
Then I'm alone for one eternal second.

Honourable Mention

JOHN SOUSTER

To John Clare

Is there indeed some other region where
    Past poets live again and see below
    How those who follow them must ever know
Such conflicts as they knew, like sorrows share?
Then look on one from your own county, Clare,
    Himself no stranger to the plough and hoe,
    One who like you has lived among the low
When rural poverty verged on despair.

Truth was the greatest quality you had
    And where truth dwells is seldom far from pain.
    Yours was a life of labour, hardship, strain,
Where little that was human made you glad.
Yet better with you to be counted mad
    Than with some other poets reckoned sane.

ANNE ASHWORTH

For Ireland

Less for the high fort,
the lonely tower, the tales
of strong Cuchulain or
the pinioned sons of Lir,
less for the swift sails,
the wild Atlantic gales

than for the soft speech,
a mild and crooning strain,
for morning-blurring mist,
fuschia and bindweed's twist,
for kind and greening rain
painting an inland plain;

less for the silver tongue
of Yeats the passionate,
less for faith held fast
in Derry or Belfast,
the bold and bidden heart
that tears a race apart

than for the small smile,
the greeting at the gate,
the "Luvly day, arl right",
the unhurried firm delight
furled in eyes: hate
finding its counterweight—

for these a rhyme to measure
a stranger's pleasure.

WINONA BAKER

The Wintering Land

In city cemetery
the pedestalled stone angel
turns her back to me
gazes at the sea

the pulp mill squeezes smoke
along the waterfront

Nanaimo's storied high-rise
built on plundered land

       looms

    phallic in fog

old-timers have predicted
it will sink or topple

the wintering land waits
for the return of gifts

DAVID BARNETT

Outback

She peers across the totem
of her grub-clan to
a eucalyptus bole,

its blaze and profile on
the oxide ground alongside
terra-cotta stones

who speak simply of
their aeons, the spells they lob
over a land that's saved

from a plague, sits
by the skies visiting
the copper in its arteries.

From her core, an air —
crepitant, tinctured —
tickles marl and snare,

cave and snake. They scrape
her with their flagrant praise,
for she, too, is able

to settle with herself
on this daybreak-swell,
where the vanes of unfledged

pelicans tremor and
a silhouette stands
in a stork's attitude.

Chirring, it hands its dream
to the gummy trees.
They sip it to relieve

her in turn. The earth
tingles as she curls
her silty feet, berthed

here in this space
with its savour raised
to the aged patience

in a spider's eyes.
A pebble rattles inside
her until she sways.

She doesn't tumble since
she's braced by a twist
of light across a ridge

and its crinkles. It spills
on her and on the wind-
shift she dabbles with

her slow-worm fingers, her scars
and her fits, the dance
of her charmed arms.

PAUL BERRY

Brandeston School Oak

You are: a visit to gran's;
a favourite armchair, comfy, worn;
the best teacher in the world.

They bring me to visit,
introduce me. You say nothing.
Me: "They have told me much about you,

the safe arbour of your branches' reach
giving time, space, a place
to reflect or speed passing guilt."

But does my wonder sound hollow —
too many winters fogging eyes
to see the God in a tree?

Or is it that, beyond the river's turn,
wounded bark screams as sawteeth cut
and wood smoke taints the air.

We kill for a full grate,
maim for a table of English oak.
What then for our children,
their cares, or birds?

MIKE BOLAND

Starlings

It was a dull, dull day;
Rain lashed in periodic blasts.
January trailed a cloak of storms,
Wind howled to the coming night,
And the sun, setting under heavy cloud
Shot out one final drawn-out flash
Of light across the sky.

A swirl of starlings flocked to roost,
Coalescing, shifting, merging,
Seeming one vast entity,
But each a single scrap of life.
They flashed in the sun like fireflies;
Each bird ashine with glory,
As if the life within
Blazed out in wonder at the world.

BRIAN BURKE

this old barn

enter this old barn
look closer than you ever had as a child
& you'll discover lead nuggets
embedded in roof & rafters
metallic shards of memory
you & your younger brother fired from a pellet rifle
at pigeons roosting

hay piled in the stalls & loft is still there
you're certain at least one straw stalk
remains from the first bale you broke

enter this old barn
lean against its frame gazing outward
survey the land like life receding
& calculate the combines
costing more than this farm did once

you sometimes wonder
if you should wish away the wheat
your father once told you
it's not a farm without a horse to feed & water
without a cow to milk & chickens underfoot
a dog for the fields & a prowling cat
a real mouser who patrols this old barn you enter

MAVIS CARTER

The Place of Wolves

She bends over the bowl
layers the papier mache
smooths with her fingertips
lets out a breath as she
looks beyond the window
to a hut with sheep skulls
tacked to the door.

The scribbled garden
slopes away to blackthorn
and the thin stream
hunting for a river.
A blackbird panic-flies
across the grass
piping its one note call.

She shivers
holds her bowl in cupped hands
as the blaze of sun
speaks to her of celebration
each tongue of flame
reaching back
leaping forward.

Windows

Woken just after five
by the clatter and scrape
of a dragged harrow
across the farmyard,
the squeal of an animal,
I lie listening to morning.

The day is unravelled mileage.
I play Chris De Burgh
dance a wild rhythm.
Across the courtyard
Jasper stalks the barn
returns, a rat in his jaws.

I stare past the window
notice mouldering leaves
and twirl a curtain ring
round one finger,
watch the rhythmic fall of rain
marking time.

In the barn electric bulbs
warm the birthing sheep.
Ewes cry out, weight the frosting air
with the musk of labour
and farm hands bend to their work.

A boy in ripped jeans tunes to Radio 1
drowns out bleating.
He rakes over the stained straw
while I turn up the volume
on Kiri Te Kanawa.

Evening and I gaze into
my neighbours' lit windows
catch glimpses of their lives.
In the firelight see my own reflection
on the darkening glass.

Chiselling the Dark

Walking in darkness to the sea
she puts chemotherapy behind her.
We measure our steps to her pace —
halfway there — she stops for breath
until a voice calls back "Oh look
the moon on the water."

The beach awash with silver
we collect driftwood, use our flares
to light a fire that sparks the sky —
settle Judith on a boulder
with shells for her lap, sea-weed
draped across her hair.

There's a light out to sea
that rises, falls on the tide,
a small scream above Cricieth.
We sit on cold pebbles, circle her —
our voices chiselling the dark.

Algarve Spring

Somewhere among Umbrella Pines
my first cuckoo of the year.
Almond trees in the wind
and white Marguerites in black shade.

    Here men shape clay around their thigh
    cut it to size, test between thumb and finger.

Motor bikes stutter along the road
to Santa Catarina, head for market;
barking dogs, cockerels, sheep on trucks,
goats tethered to fence posts.

    Tiles fired in orange kilns, are stacked
    row on row. Men, red with dust, rough-handed.

Orchards heavy with oranges
thick with juice. I pick one
hold it in my palm
and slowly breath in.

R.L. COOK

At Cunninghill

At Cunninghill the earth was sprouting children,
Strong, running stems; flowers that laughed and fled,
Flashing, through grass: bright seed of benevolent dragons,
Risen from soil, crashing old winter's barriers,
Into the high blue, sky-blue
Boundless halls of spring.

On Sunday, Easter Sunday,
At Cunninghill the field was ringing with
The bells of youth; the world grew gay; the shadow
Of the atom's menacing mushroom was forgotten,
Its darkness rolled away. Among the clover,
With cleaving cries,

Out of the womb of earth they spiralled
Under the whorling clouds that, driven, driving,
Scudded across the smooth, unthreatening sky,
Marbling that giant, far-off, concave eggshell
Of heaven with moving fleeces, where a lark
Hovered and carolled.

At Cunninghill there bloomed another Eden
Peopled with children. The deep force of earth,
Its primitive simplicity flowed through
Their veins all afternoon and, when time's shadow
Edged them away out of the field to wander
Along the road to home,

They changed — were quiet, suddenly, and human.
Licked by the sun's warm tongue they drowsed to bed,
Haloed with dreams of running air and tumbling
Back to the earth's own rhythm.

       May they still
Keep through the years some of the light they found,
Today, at Cunninghill.

BARBARA CRUPI

Flamenco

In swirls of light
the dance was born
castanets beat their tattoo,
colour was formed;

Lilac haze of havana cigars
incensed the air,
the man and the girl —
(no-one else was there)
— twined and intertwined, yet untouching.

We clapped and breathless, held our breath,
bound in a rhythmic spell.

We threw our pesetas
and loot collected, cuban heeled, yet tiny,
his black eyes no longer glittering,
— light guttered —
he shrank shadow thin
against the wall.

That night, dream-like, I danced:
an entranced gypsy girl.

MARGUERITE DOLSEN

The Calligrapher

Silent, alone, squared off
before the graph, prepared,
head bent, eyes intent,
bonded to the task.
The sure prehensile hand
forwards in rhythm subtly slow
an ancient craft, a legacy
centuries before the Gutenbergs.
Caress of ink
on curve and curl of letters
where meaning born of words is cradled,
and when the pen is laid aside,
a message, beautifully given.

GERALD ENGLAND

Clinging to the Valley

screes of shale
remain where
slag-heaps rose

the machinery
and the railway line
are gone

banks of bleak homes
some boarded up
seem to slope nowhere

in the Station Cafe
they laugh and gossip
tell tales of holidays
and how nice it is
to get back

rain streams
relentlessly
on rows of pigeon lofts

over the mountain
where the last
driftmine
still works
life takes wing

IAN ENTERS

Aphrodite in July

Fruit hangs on a salt tree.
Gunmetal sea salivates lead
In the tearless eye of sun.

Fat birds strew guano offering
With gull mew. Bone earth
Grows straight trunks
Palming the sky.

Orange she stretches.
Her underarms are white
Under the cliff.

She is whirlpool drawn,
Hearing heart tides,
Willing a blue dawn,
Oiling the groyne
Where shadowed arrows slide.

KATHERINE L. GORDON

November Storm

Bare-stripped, blackened branches
Were lashed by the wind last night,
Their winter penance
For sweet summer excess begins.
Trees arched beaten backs
Against the wind-whips,
Twig sharding the shifting sky
In wooden agony,
Tapping for any source of mercy
On the windowed walls.
The moon flashed electric shocks
Between black driven clouds,
Lighting the writhing tree limbs
Or shrouding all in flickering strobe
Of cloud-black and moon-white.
I lie jolted between the flickers,
Between pain ending and pain beginning,
Purgatory of the wooden heart.
Astral fingers tear at the shredded sky,
Seeking the sacred space
Beyond all winter storms.

DAVID A. GROULX

Penemue and the Indians

We are the ghosts
of our grandfathers
and grandmothers

we are life lived again

We are the knot
between the past and the future
we are string
binding our grandfathers
to our grandchildren

RICHARD M. GROVE

February Evening Sky

There is hope on the horizon,
with our setting sun,
5:05 pm,
the amber beam of her brilliance,
still unset,
inches from disappearing,
over the blanketed silver hills,
of the still winter landscape.
Minutes later,
Venus and Saturn,
bright in the western sky.
Venus in her brilliant glory.
Saturn, a pin prick,
saddled fatefully beside her wonderment.
Both reflecting the sun's now set resplendence.

ALISTAIR HALDEN

Fulmars

Love, let us cease this chatter, and observe.
You are in fulmar country.
No doubt the word you would have used is "seagulls".
But look!
A few quick wing-beats,
And then a muscle stiffens for the glide.
When did you see a gull that flew like that?

If we should clamber, toes on crumbling rock,
Our fingers clutching clumps of wiry tussock,
Towards their ledge,
We would discern the nostrils on their bills —
And we would keep our distance.

Now listen!
Hear how they talk in guttural clicks and clacks,
Relating to each other what they see
And fear —
Their commentary on the state of things.

And here we are,
Perched between sea and sky,
Another mating couple,
Surveying the puppet world so far below,
And clacking at each other.

I hold your slender body
Irrationally tight,
Lest, as my muscle stiffens,
You should launch yourself away
With three quick heartbeats.

MARGARET B. HAMMER

High-Rise Mondrian

Squares of Caribbean colour
balance in the dark
apartment block
like sharp notes sounded
in an hour of silence.

Dancers jerk and writhe
in the yellow box.
A stoop-shouldered housewife,
against green,
dries the final dish.
Bathrobed, two forgetful figures
crisscross the cerise.

In the orange square
a black cutout
leans, statue-still,
against the window frame.

Suddenly he lifts
a trumpet to his lips,
turns straight towards me
and blows one high, clear note
against the grey walls
of my cell.

F.R. HARRIS

We Had Our Targets

(1943)

Plundering along that lane
to Finningley, the nests
were April-loaded, like planes
in the aerodrome.

Greedy for eggs, we drew blood,
cursed the hedge, as birds
and Lancasters took flight
for trees and Frankfurt.

Life oozed
through pierced shells fragile
in death; for it was war
and we had our targets.

Glad, we nursed our spoils
in cotton-wool; sang
in a Yorkshire spring, though
fewer birds would sing.

And later, on the news,
we'd hear of cities bombed,
Life destroyed, and airmen missing,
cancelling our joys.

DAVID HILLEN

Suddenly

Suddenly
one cool, sunny afternoon
across the distance of hurt
through the noise of our voices
we make peace — easily
— suddenly.

MARY HODGSON

Saybrook Point, Connecticut

Maps particularise
for those who wish to be precise
about place,
but the sea washes all shores
is not nice, does not fuss,
ignores such pettiness
as names, boundaries
and difference
of territories.

Here at Saybrook
the land has ground
to shingle, into sand
as at other places;
the groins reach out
to check the drift
the shift
of sand-grist down the shore,
which I have seen before
on other beaches.
Here
I might be at home
alone on sand-stretch
freshed by wind
etched by the lace-edged
fretting water, the flecked
and salt-grit air, the corrugated
sea.

Which sea?
the green-grey waves don't say,
surge unspecific
from horizon to horizon,
horizon to shore,
suggest no zone, no name
offer no bond;
the map alone makes claim
with unseen lines
to parcel out dominion,
delimit land and ocean —
tells me I stand
(at home here)
in New England
on edge of Long Island Sound.

Peter and the Boys

He taught my boys to gut fish,
glittering blue-black mackerel
straight from the sea,
striped bellies gleaming silver like
moons behind prison bars.
They fetched a flat stone and
bucket of clear water;
he showed his sharp knife,
blade whetted keen enough
so he said
to slice cobweb,
then delicately slit and opened flesh
like an envelope,
scooped entrails out.

They washed the body,
turned it wonderingly in their hands
stroking the smooth scales,
inspected the inside and
ran their fingers round
to ensure the cavern clean;
then each in turn took next fish
and the next,
held the sharp knife a reverent moment
and, copying him precisely,
plunged in the point,
gutting for themselves
and us
that first supper.

Elderberry Harvest

It seems prosaic enough, utilitarian even
(we turn the berries into wine)
with routine time and place,
always the early autumn and that same muddy lane.
We go armed — a long thick pole, slotted together
(we take screwdriver and screws)
with hand-made hook on the end — not a frail weapon.
We wear wellingtons or thick-soled boots, old clothes.
I cannot do with gloves so my hands get torn
and stained, grubby under the finger-nails with dye
that marks me out for days.

This year someone had been there first.
The earth was churned, some
red-ribbed stalks were skeletons —
stripped by birds? —
but a tree of easy access rudely pillaged,
boughs broken, leafage torn, fruit squashed on ground,
suggested youngsters' clutching, plundering,
though the raw fruit is sour.
                                      We purposed more;
surveyed for best fruit, set to work.
We hooked the branches down and sank
into sharp dank smell of elder,
our faces thrust among rough undersides of leaves
close to the spotted bark.
Small opaque spiders hung on threads
in the snapshot second, stick insects froze,
winged mites whizzed furious war-dance as we closed
deliberately on plump ripe berries
drooping with heavy promise, hand cupped under
the rounded cluster of fruit, clasping our grail.

Berries and dark bark stigmatise the fingers.
Hard sharp branches scratch, gouge
as they leap back, released.
The harvest of perfection leaves
scars.

PETER HOWARD

Love Letter to Brigitte Helm

(Star of the film Metropolis,
directed in 1926 by Fritz Lang.)

How did you manage it, to play both parts,
both sides of woman it's no longer correct
even to think about? They were metaphors:
the virgin chased by a gloved hand that,
in self-inflicted deformity, no longer feels,
and the most seductive robot wink
in cinema history, out of control,
leading troglodyte saps in ridiculous sabots
to near destruction, inciting dinner-suits
to fisticuffs, murder, suicide,
laughing as the flames of the witch-pyre
lick her to base metal.

Most think that science died, became Death rather,
(despite her ability since then to provide
whiter than white lab coats for acolytes)
at Trinity in '45. Fritz Lang anticipated the event
two decades earlier, burning you on film
the year Baird fumbled in Soho with his discs,
demonstrating dim images of your medium's decline.

Rewind two hundred years, Sir Isaac's light,
celebrated by Pope, is nearly spent.
Such is the afterglow, there's enough for all,
even for Joseph Wright to fill, from a hidden source,
(but we know what it is) the staring eyes,
the first mad scientist's wild medusa hair,
his guests collusive, even the boy
who doesn't care, even the thoughtful,
disapproving frown, too civilised to smash
the dying bird's glass prison, or at least walk out.
Only the girl, who knows enough to know it's wrong,
won't watch, won't hear quiet, glib sophistries,
can save us with her innocence, it seems.

King George reins over this: the orreries,
air pumps, electric shocking public lectures;
then he goes mad. Modern Prometheus walks on,
and science falls apart. Everything's relative,
light is neither on the one hand
nor the other. John Squire shouts down Pope.
Hawking, from his chair, plucks an arrow,
twists it in spiteful knots and fractures it, so
we don't know where we're going any more, nor when.
We yearn for certainties of gold and mystery,
want labs to be like those we learned at school:
Keep Out until omniscient Teacher permits
entry to familiar mahogany and brass.

Brigitte, you played two stereotypes:
the witch-whore who can't deliver (we noted
the conspicuous absence of a metallic cunt)
and the science-taming maid. We're horrified.
Nasty white scientists wriggling into nature,
scrap the sky-screwing Saturn V and design
a womb called the shuttle. It's a feeble excuse,
a crude setting up of a straw analogy.
Science isn't sex. We're simply afraid of it,
detest its insistence that we grow up
and keep on growing. We want Mummy
to tell us it's safe: Lang knew better
than to let you play that part. We don't.
So we keep the *Principia* out of print, remind ourselves
Newton was an alchemist, as if that made a point.
In this we've regressed since '26, no longer sure
if we want to play with a hundred and something elements,
and if we weren't happier with four.

WINIFRED N. HULBERT

Manitoba Farmers

Three trucks
    three colours
ton-and-a-half
tarpaulined
    like cows heavy in calf
    filing from the field
    snorting under the strain
three trucks
roar from the bin
round the curve
and slowly halt
    halfway down
        the gently sloping lane.

The drivers alight
    a team
checking for trouble signs.
Frosted shouts echo:
    "How's that tire?"
    "This tarp's all right."
Men and motors
breathe steam.

Mounted again
the men
manoeuvre the sharp turn
space themselves on the open road
    snow-packed
increasing speed:
    giant bumble bees
    in droning flight.

Each
piloting this precious load
    of mustard seed
to the far-off cleaning mill
feels a faint flutter
    in his weathered breast:
the old excitement his forefathers felt
piloting prairie schooners
    laden with their all
across this vast expanse
    of untamed West.

The challenge
    of those wooden wheels
is rumbling still
in stout hearts
    light with neighbourly goodwill.

SHEILA HYLAND

Summer Daze

Sister! your voice calls
whispering in corn husks
swishing the barley pearls

Here it comes, scrambling
down the blackberry hedge
spidering the strawberry patch
prickling cane of raspberry
It stays spiking cornflower blue!

Remember those huge bouquets
we picked for Sister Therese?
And how the blue liquid
dripped from your eye
brilliant, shining!

Do you weep for the days
we didn't spend together?
You too busy with friends,
little sis, too green to grow
the longing unheard, unsaid

How did those months grow into moons
and melt you into silver
my brilliant, shining June!

LAURA H. KENNEDY

Leaving Ash Creek

I think we were cowboys once, you know
as like calls out to like . . .
it was a beginning
perfect and primitive,
wild hope under darkening sky —
we took a step and fell
into a canyon of
a thousand fallen stars.

Once, I gave you broken things:
blue glass bottles of dreams,
arrows,
the moon a chandelier
of antler and bone
branded on the night,
prairie for miles
beyond whorls of tangled, barbed wire
and weathered wood.

MARY KRATT

At the Mercury Mill

Our three room house
belonged to the mill.
We filled it.
Mother. Four children.
Father had gone.
She worked the spinning room
at the front of the mill.
We stayed by ourselves, but
felt her watching
from the mill window.

We knew not to cross
those railroad tracks or
climb the water tank. She
showed us how to do.
Her boss let her come
at 9:00 and noon and 3:00
long enough to nurse the baby.
For $2.20 a day
her shift was eleven hours.
At nights she cooked
and washed and ironed. Then
she got sick.

I was twelve,
two years too young by law
to work, but the doctor
changed my age on the paper
and I swept floors
at the mill,
piles of lint, until
they found out, until
she got well.
I remember
that mill.

Widow

At the funeral
surrounded,
as family fills
that space
beside her, she
lifts her eyes —
the raw, sudden
stare of one
who's lost
her skin.

Kinfolk

To have them, there must be somebody
    left, somebody with name, blood, strain of traits —
    hairy back, eyes set close,
    Uncle Arthur had no toes.

Johnny'd stain a whole shirt with sweat, barely moving
    or he'd lean over a family album to say,
    those ears, just like Ed's
    or that little crooked finger.

Rose wears long pants all her life,
    because at a cousin's once, she heard
    behind a kitchen door, somebody say too loud
    don't you think she's got Aunt Alma's piano legs?

And as for talkers,
    Cy made the simplest story
    a winding country road,
    crooked as a dog's hind leg.

If you don't have generations,
    don't have children,
    or if you've just one son
    and he went out for cigarettes
    and someone shot him walking to a Circle K
    where would all this go?

A person needs three
        one for him
    one for her
        one for them.
One in these times of guns,
    fire, wreck or war,
    riot or dire disease,
    is goin' to get it.
He'll die. She won't come home.
Who'll buy the photo album tossed
    to the flea market?

Aunt Hazel wasn't kin.
She had no kids. She loved my parents
    and later me.
In the photo album my husband says,
    who's that? She looks like you.
More than blood gets passed along.

Factory Whistles, Early 1900s, North Carolina

Up here
on the hill farm,
hoeing,
I hear them whistles plain
down
in that far town,
factory whistles
calling.

In our high fields
I've done my share
of killing hogs,
hauling, picking,
plowing, all this
men's work
and women's too
in a family plumb full
of daughters.

Down there's people
I've not met,
a job that pays,
a new dress, and maybe
a road to somewhere.
I'm 17.
I run away with the hired hand
to keep from plowing.

CECIL JUSTIN LAM

Morning Report

Postal Strike
TTC Strike
Civic Worker, strike
I strike
One to infinity
In the mood
The Nation
Falls into tears
Crocodile superior
Turtle complex
Lizard tongue

JOHN B. LEE

The Coal Miners

The one coal miner says
he loved his work
says, he knelt
like a priest at prayer
all day
and played his banjo spade so hard
his hands bled black
to keep the coke clear
of the hungry drill
and you could tell there was truth
in what he'd said
his eyes luminous
with the soft brown light
of muddy rivers in them
and though he coughs into his hand
a sad confession of black dust
he says, if he hadn't been laid off
in 87 he'd be there still
with his methane lamp held to the wall
mothering the fever from the air
moiling under the weight of the mountain
with his crew of cousins
knowing you dare not let a stranger down
to the face of the dig
for fear he wasn't worth saving.

And his brother on the engine
brags with his moustache
the stiff curl of it waxed
wisely up as if
it shared a feature with the woody ferns
of a well-made fiddle.
Oh, he was a man of fashion
a sense of his important self
given to the space he filled
though he was short and rather round
in boots and hard hat
he was real to the very core
like good coal, pure and proud
if you crossed him
he'd have cured your error with his eyes
as a dog cures sheep
their odd stray intentions
becoming true to his.
No one would die on his shift.
You knew by the look of him
he'd dig a chimney to the sky
and breathe the moon.

The Winter of 96

> *and so, confusing density and destiny*
> *all the buoyant angels*
> *shatter on the ground*
> *like brittle glass*

His heart a stone inside a stone
they found the homeless man
frozen in the February street
stuck to that clean sunlit city morning
like the gelid winter jetsam
lost rivers leave on land.
And over days indoors
he sagged into such sorrow
his hands relaxing their blue grip
his face-flesh like wet paper
his cryogenic heart easing its valves
into cardiograms of ice.
And he was nameless and
unmourned, the same glacial oddity
carried by multitudes in snow-swept mountains
nosing into their valleys
with the cold curiosity of ages.
He died into the evening
like a second darkness
then died again, slacking
in the morgue
lightless pools of inner night
seeking the middle state of water.

I Think Continually of Those Who Are Truly Average

for Stephen Spender, a reply

I think continually of those
who are truly average
who live out their lives
loving their days
who in death
inhabit the landscape
the same as us all
under a slow sighing down
of soil
like the exhale of a green sleeper
and are remembered
over the fading recollection
of one decade, perhaps two
and then forgotten, entirely
save for a few pale photographs.

And if the gods
who measure the value of a life
set that mind against the sages
that soul against the saints
they'd find in the balance of smoke
and in the aristocracy of the human heart
there are no meaningless fires.
The love of each friend
is like a barn burning in the wind.

ANNE LEWIS-SMITH

Isandlwana

It was still there
— the hate.
that huge empty ochre
grassland
with hollows where
twenty thousand waited,
shaking the ground
with bare feet
stamping the sound,
the rhythmic
suck of breath
hiss of death
still in the wind.

Leaving, we were
suddenly surrounded
by children where
none had been,
driving a herd of goats
across our tracks.

Blocking our way back.

We locked ourselves in our car.
Young Zulus, unsmiling,
came closer, milling
round, thin arms waving
thicker sticks.

A stone was thrown.

We drove fast —
away from echoes
of the past,
bumping unevenly
across dry veld
till thankfully,
we reached the road.

— the hate
is still there.

Widow

There are ghosts in her eyes.

When the turf fell flaming in the hearth
I saw them leap to life.
In her eyes the wall writhed red
and she outside it in the fiery dark,
that through four thousand nights
has nightmared down her sleeping hell.

The lake flamed blood that once
and every shepherds sunset bleeds again,
twisting the knife,
blazing the cottage roof.

— and through the years
her husband's screams
murder her ears.

NOAH LEZNOFF

the wind is blowing me away!

that's what we take turns yelling our arms spread running
across the field, my daughter and I,
the wind is blowing us away
though my feet plod
in the manner of a wooden-legged giant
in fairness to a three-year-old's chasing
so I may play and seem to run, arms
pin-wheeling, head back
    the movie "whoooaaa" rising above the field and
wind we chase each other on, save each other
from flying over
    like cilia of dandelion seed
and running
(the wind is blowing me away)
    against the tugging on my jacket: "Don't worry Dada,
I'm saving you!"

teacher

It gets dark at four
now, I am talking
with the difficult boy,

and these low explicit clouds
make the sky a marble table
to stand under, our elbows

resting on the Mercury fence
that divides school from
the ravine

Here, where I can smoke and
he can swear, we explain ourselves

becoming simple, our voices
astonishingly soft

In Moonlight After Rain

— after a scape by F.H. Varley

At the foot of a landscape cleaving
where everything's so darn blue
and aqua and teal and white,
and the tree-thick mountains hang wet,
and the sky, lots of it, seems washed in
quiet affliction —
at the foot of all this
a small figure crossing a bridge,
an earth-clot shadow in a hat.

It is moonlight after rain,
mud and the texture of needles,
the ferrous smell of damp rock
and the human heading bent

toward the middle ground: an island up-cropping
black-green, two tall pines that
spire, lean away from each other like
lovers keeping stubborn silence.

Around, around, around, or through?

So much freedom for a shadow!
a blue mountain, a firmament spreading,
a thousand heirs to light and rain,
and that distance into which, when we open
our night eyes, we are always walking

MICHAEL LONDRY

What Makes You Feel You Are Suited to This Type of Employment?

Because, despite my appearance, I have the strength
of twenty men.

Because all the events and experiences of my life
have brought me here, in this moment, to this place, this
colonnaded hall, this mahogany desk.

Because I am a sort of volcano of productivity and success,
ready to blow.

Because I am an avid scholar of French Absurdist theatre
of the 1890's — especially *Ubu*.

Because I highly value personal freedom and creativity,
and dislike any form of routine or time-pressure.

Because my bones become soft and pliable
at the sight of beauty.

Because I understand thoroughly the mechanics of the
rise and fall of civilizations, and have brought my wrench.

Because last night, under the pale light of the first quarter
moon, my wife and I made love in the woods behind the
house — first like animals, then slow and sweet.

Because on a clear day I can still see from my balcony
the shining towers of Constantinople rising up from
morning mist.

Because I am an enemy of the Regime.

Because there is no antidote to the charm of my smile.

Because I will promise not to woo your daughters.

Because I can sing you to sleep.

HUGH MacDONALD

The Digging of Deep Wells

involves
the breaking of solid ground,
stacking a circle's worth of sod
between tree stumps,
shovelling layers
of damp and musty clay,
into wooden pails,
and soon requires
a ladder, and a tripod
of white-barked birch,
and where it's joined
a wooden block
through which passes
a hundred feet
of sturdy rope.
Then begins
the lining of walls
— fresh cut sandstone
starts ten feet down,
builds up layer by layer
tight to the top.
Since there's no sign yet
of gurgling water,
the digger digs anew
goes down inside
the present ring of rock
with short armed spade,
sharp and heavy crow,
hammers stubborn aggregate
smashing layered shale,
load after deadly load
sways up behind the rope.
The lower he goes,
the harder falling pebbles hit,
the deeper the darkness.

At ladder's full length
more layered circles of stone,
hole gradually widening
until this present wall
provides foundation
for the wall above
and by lantern light
the digger stands
on broken rock,
watches the ladder rise
and disappear above the rim.
The air is chill:
each clatter of crow
each scrape of shovel
each claustrophobic breath
echoes up the hole
toward the light
past the rain of dust
that coats the chilling sweat
of neck and brow.
And now at end of work
the bucket ends its day,
is swift unbound,
replaced by bosun's chair,
twirling he rises, to sleep
and then descend again
and again
until one afternoon
he stands in icy damp
hears the gush of stream
and fresh cold water rise up,
shock his weary groin.
Filled up with sudden joy
he risks to look
at what's above
and finds as his reward
a perfect circus of stars

Behind the Red Brick House
Charlottetown, P.E.I. 1955

Doctor Joe and Colin
and the twins
stand in soggy sleeves
behind their house
They lay the water down
in shining pools
night after night
and on frost crisp mornings
break up shells
of tinkle ice
that mar the thickening surface
then melt it down
with steaming floods
and leave for office and school
impatient for the work to end

Soon come nights
when hordes of children
shove inside the changing shed
fill lungs with kerosene charged air
or sit and wheeze
and tie their skates
on ice-lump mounds
along the edge

Captains toss
an out-of-season bat
pick shouting teams
and nets are coats
or husks of snow
With eyes like young owls
we stick handle
around figure-skating girls
and flirting pairs
"no lifties" is the rule
but pucks still fly
we scramble over banks
and mine mounds of drift

We play til toes are trapped
laces locked in hanging icicles
We're never more awake
than when we leave
and crunch along streets
sticks across shoulders
hobo style
our skates
lace-hung and steaming
at our backs
and once in bed
we sleep so fast
and dream
of how we'll play
the next game
and the next

TANIS MacDONALD

Service with a Smile

among the crash and clatter of dishes,
always a spot of gravy on my white cuff,
displeasing the green-eye-shadowed
new deli manager who didn't know
how to speed order pick-up,
couldn't tell a good pickle from bad,
couldn't even find the words to tell me
my earrings were too big, blossoming
blue sparklers during the dinner shift,
I carried corned beef and cabbage
to a ten-table section while she struggled
to choose the proper managerial phrase
and I loaded plates up my arm and
pretended I had no idea what
the problem was

at midnight, so foot-swollen and bone-sore
my back a series of grinding cracks
in the corner booth where I emptied
my apron of sour money and filmy credit slips,
I smelled of mustard even on my days off,
and my boyfriend lost his head one night
and heaved a whole tray of glasses at
the Portuguese grill cook, fifteen transparent
missiles exploded on the grill, showered
slivers on the cook's curled back,
but the cook was a decent guy
and never took it out on me,
my orders up fresh and hot,
every time

COLIN MACKAY

Bosnian Elegy

The day came up with darkness.
Fires paled, but the smoke
hung over the ruins,
and out of the smoke came things
we had wanted to forget.
The dead lay in their wet shadows.
There were so many.
Under the bridge, where
the broken tree had fallen,
they lay tangled in its branches,
a dam of rotting flesh,
and the water swelled around them
until the stream burst its banks
and flooded the path
where cattle had gone, breathing gently,
in the day of long ago,
and the pastureland
sprinkled with cowpats,
and the football pitch with the old
broken goalposts,
and the lovers' bushes
warm with passion.
The water followed them all
drowning their tracks
in the cold green,
and only our staring eyes
were dry.

When we came away from that place
we walked unsteadily
with creaking limbs and the shiver
of ice-water in our veins.
> *Silence under the beech trees,*
> *silence we can never forget!*

When we came away from that place
homes lay out on the street,
all the doors stood open
in the breaking mouth of dawn.
> *Silence under the oak trees,*
> *silence we can never forget!*

When we came away from that place,
when we came away,
its strange fruit came with us
staining our souls.
> *Silence under the pine trees,*
> *silence we can never forget!*

Men of the black mountains,
of the tumbling rivers
and rushing skies!
Women of the white walls
and red tile roofs,
of the mosque and minaret!
Children of the forests and cliffs,
of the Bogomils, Tito
and the partisan war!
People like any other
who watch television
and walk together and laugh
in the twilight!

Over your pretty villages
the smoke hangs now,
your white walls
are hacked with bullets
and stained with blood.
We have seen your children
dancing in the flames,
your men festooned
with bullets and hand-grenades,
and your women raped by the dozen.

We shut our doors
because we did not want to hear the weeping,
we shut our ears, our hearts, our minds
because we did not want to hear the weeping,
but the weeping seeped through
like rainwater,
like the clouds' tears,
like the grief of heaven,
and soon nothing could be heard
but the weeping.
Now, Bosnia,
your silence
is my life.
Your grief pursues me
and I see your blood
dripping from the mournful sky.
Every day I see the smoke
of your many burnings.
When the sun goes down
your passion
wears a crown of flames.

Bosnian Village

By the banks of the Drina
the pale village floats beneath the moon
and the muddy river turns its pebbles
into treasure.
At night the workfield is hidden.
At night the smell of it
sinks back into the old wood,
and along the stony path
come the village heifers
in a heavy scent of byres
and warm straw.
At night, this night,
only the owl hunts
in the moon-way, in the time
of small screams.
The night is soft with the stain
of forgetfulness.
The smell is only of farmyards
and permitted killing.

Tomorrow boys will fish corpses from the stream.

JOHN MARKS

Bosnia

all those hatreds
back in action
like
iced familiars

cold objects
gripped by god knows what
certainties

thawed on the heat
of bodies
smashed in the eyes of children,

icons
waving in the glare of air
sultry and mild
atrophied by the dust of centuries

sunlight stipples
the pock-marked churches-turned-mosques
turned-churches-turned-mosques
as blitz-hardened women
spill out their venom
a little at a time

is there no breaking-out of this thin space,
trapped in this time and place,
the shell-shocked buildings
tumbling right back to Constantinople?

dawn deformed by the lurid skies
and men's eyes,
glazed by the fires of time

look through this enemy air,
staring into the future
seeing only the past.

JOY MARTIN

Night of the Gale

The house groans tonight
its beam-bones creak, brittle-tempered.
Outside the gusting wind
shredding the last leaves from the shaken trees
dances destruction through the garden,
lashes the window panes
with spiteful spears of rain.
Curled embryonic beneath my duvet
within this womb of a house
which has become my refuge
nothing can touch me,
yet the lifting tiles and straining stairs
tell me how fragile is safety,
how a wrong word on a wild night
can tumble communicating walls,
and a turning away
loosen the strong cement of loving.
Tentatively I touch your sleeping form,
make sure of your nearness
and lull myself, security assumed,
into a transient calm, knowing it may be
merely the eye of the storm.

CATHERINE McCAUSLAND

No Pilot Required

I stood,
lined up under
the lead lights,
a beacon
drawing you
into my harbour.

A pair of lights
    drawing you into my sheltered pleasures.
A pair of lights
    found by your searching eyes.

Through the Narrows,
that difficult passage
of closely set outcroppings
and stirred up waters,
you line up
the pair of lights
guiding your
safe return,
easing you into
my generous comfort —
a homecoming.

JANE McCREERY

Turnpike World Series

I could be listening to Carpenters' music
or those carbohydrate-drugged voices
that phone into talk shows condemning
school strikes, other people's abortions.
But instead I follow the sixth game
on stations fading out and fading back,
as I speed through Nowhere, Pennsylvania,
with nobody in the seat beside me.

A familiar voice (one I associate
with Gillette razor blades) pronounces
names I attached faces to: Hernandez,
Stanley, Gedman, Boggs, Darling, Romero.
Orange lights glow on the dashboard —
my little homefire. And in another state
55,000 drunks howl, "Mookie!" The roar
mixes with static to fill up the car.

This is when the unforgiving will accuse
the Red Sox of choking again. Religious
Mets fans will name it "God's Will."
The ball I'm imagining takes a wild hop,
right past Buckner, as my white Pontiac
hurtles through the blue-black night.
It's over. Everybody can head for home,
calling tomorrow One-Last-Chance.

DERRICK McINTOSH

Proverb of Poverty

Sometimes —
that time after
sunset
on an overcast
night —
Someone —
that one that
cannot be seen after
sunset —
walks on gravel
in the gray summer
light.

Maybe that one is one
still waiting for
the meteors
who remembers what shooting stars
are when they flash,
the tail of a g
meeting the peak of an h,
in the night
in the summer light
in the hand
that someone writes.

The universe,
though,
is cold in the sky;
searching for quasars
is no longer permitted.
Work must be begun.

Hypocrisy demands a factory
to forge granite,
igneous
though the rock may be,
to cut trees
and to burn the dead;
a sixteen-hour day
and children without limbs.

Two centuries of slavery
have been imported tonight.
No one knows that Winnipeg
strikes tonight.
Strolling across gravel
is loneliness tonight
as Canada contemplates
forgetting,
as Canada embraces
the Proverbs of Poverty,
as someone stalks
across gravel tonight
and cannot see the constellations
in the wintry light . . .
        on the faucet
ice grows tight.

ELISE McKAY

No Miracle

It startled us, that Easter,
walking on the hill.
A long climb
and then a level track.
On each side sheets of rain
fell white against black crags
but we held safe,
a middle way.

It startled us;
water, blue like lapis lazuli,
glinted in black heather.
There was no miracle,
only the shock of light and shade,
and joy —
simple as water
lying on the hill.

The Ammonite

He took the fossil gingerly
and held it in his hand.
It was too hard
for his ten years to comprehend.
I thought he'd ask, how old?
Instead, "What was it like — alive?"
I tell him "It was curled and soft,
could feel, like you."

His hand in answer tightens round the stone,
as though he tried to force the meaning through.
No use; his grasp uncurls,
he loses interest, hands it back.
But I have seen the fossil imprint
on his palm. Three million years
to make this one soft mark.

HILARY MELLON

Marbled Moon

We are making moons today:
the play dough is marbled,
swirling with strange colours.

My daughter pretends dinner:
serving blue peas onto a red plate,
she carefully adds a marbled moon.

"Eat it, Mummy" she says
"with the yellow spoon."

CHAD NORMAN

Wall Against the Back

for Dorothy Livesay

Being alive, air accepted, the steps complete,
being what's aged into a gift,
what was & remains so quick,

Life.

As if the sperm & ovum are to blame.
As if the Fruit & Serpent shared a Garden.
As if the Bang was any louder that a snap.
As if the journey could be other than mystery.

Life.

Has there been a size for all the missing,
for the forgettings? A measure? A gauge?
And what about wonder, is it new,
being closer to death than birth?
Is it even wonder?

(It must be!
Forgive me, I know little; I still stare
at skin left to look like gathered ashes.)

And days, what days are special: those
when family reads you poems you have written?

(Of course I know little.
Just that Earth,
our shared stone,
will remember your Living

MARY NUGENT

Rievaulx Abbey
(AD 1978)

Pigeon brothers,
perched high on ruined walls,
chant matins through the winter silence;
clinking hammers add descant
and honking geese
a distant angelus.

Discordant crows,
circling the dark wood,
caw in monotones,
momentarily breaking the pastoral peace
of a remote religious order,
preserved through lost centuries.

A black-robed nun
rakes up brown leaves
in sleeping garden of nearby cottage,
like an undertaker
caring for his dead,
giving service to the living.

Across the fields
two white goats,
mother and kid,
munching and milking,
mark out a smallholding
nestling in the land's immensity.

Men in denim overalls
work cheerfully;
one with pipe and knitted cap
of monkshood blue —
more practical than
monkish hoods of old.

No tourists
but ourselves,
and only scaffolding to mar
an ancient abbey's beauty,
confirming man's essential part
in the eternal.

MARGARET PAIN

Dawn Watch

The night has
made its statement.
All dark long
you walked in cities
far from us and strange,
on a lonely road
and under unfamiliar stars;
we could not follow you —
or only go part way
with held hands gently pressed.

Through all the stale shut hours
your face was like a mirror;
we could see only death,
in self-reflecting
anxious images.

Now the world has turned.
Glory tops
a firtree bough
between black lines
of hill and cloud.

Dawn sky breaks
into pale rivers,
lakes of blue . . .
and look —
on the ridge
the trees have come alive,
brightness shines
through leaf and branch,
and in the wind,
storm-gulls raise wings
and fly like shuttles,
hurtled from dark to light.

PEGGY POOLE

Needlewoman

Walking past her was like
braving barbed wire
her mouth a line of pins
her breast a bush of needles;
she came to do the sewing
and always made me feel that,
cold and precise as the scissors she used,
her sharp eye appraising
from the landing window-seat,
she could stitch me into better shape.

Her husband would come swathed
in black veils when our bees swarmed.
She kept him away from other men
on our road, forbad him drink,
even their house stood aloof.
Consolation lay in wood
in building cupboards, bird tables,
and a replica of our rambling home
each stair correct, it stands now as I write
outside my room.

There were no children; he was
her child with his round pink face
and trusting blue eyes. Called Tom
his surname suggesting he was a shadow
of someone Else. I never knew her name,
cannot see her as a laughing bride,
she was too prim ever to stand undressed.

Respectability was the God to whom
she gave allegiance all her days.

BARBARA RENNIE

Au Moulin de la Galette—
Renoir has afterthoughts—

> 'Renoir's painting of weekend revellers at the open-air dance hall of that name in Montmartre could break the world record for a work of art.'
> — The Times

> 'It is to be auctioned in America with an estimate of $40 million to $50 million (£24 million to £30 million).'
> — The Daily Telegraph, 17 Jan. 90

I have the impression someone has
got something a little out of proportion.
I do not understand their dollars, or
English pounds, or people who will
pay millions of them for my *Moulin
de la Galette*, what amounts after all,
to no more than impressions of happiness
and of laughter, lovingly set down
it is true, but no more than the fleeting
captured for an instant. If I had been
able to write a cheque to settle
all my embarrassments, post-dated till
the end of the Twentieth Century . . .

Maybe I should have been always too drunk
to paint. Maybe my friends would have
carried me back to my studio, instead
of helping to lug the canvas each day
to the Moulin and to shoulder each evening
my impression of those smiling girls, swaying
with the music, in their draped and bustled gowns
as they danced, casting glances at all
those young men, there to watch them. Maybe
the music and the whispering would not
be there in the colour and the brush-strokes.

Maybe I should not have caught it at all.

> * Au Moulin de la Galette *was sold at Sotheby's, New York, on 16th May 1990, for the price of $78.1 million (£46.5 million).*

LOUISE ROGERS

Entering Cold Woodlands

Comes at dusk
a disturbing cry, on and on,
as of a young bird startled,
but winter is no time
for fledgelings.

Though cautious our approach
through ferns, a fluttering whirl
and two large birds, distracted,
fly low away. Flashes of white
reveal their anxious flight.

Many times before may they
have called out loudly and long.
How many times after
again and again
and I not hear them?

Here is a secret place
and the wanderer, where dearly
he would wish to be a friend,
remains a trespasser.

That strange cry,
how it haunts me.

K.V. SKENE

Learning Death

> *. . . if I should die before I wake,*
> *I pray the lord my soul to take.*
> (children's prayer)

I knew the facts of death
before I knew the facts of life,
squeezed their skinny bones
inside my skin; sucked air
through soggy lungs, breath after breath
breaking — like 'London Bridge',
          — like riding a nightmare heart
full stop. I knew
this — but I needed a lie. I
still shut my eyes and whisper:
safety, love,
forgiveness,
before I sleep.

DEIRDRE ARMES SMITH

Woman of Inishmaan

(Inishmaan — a lonely island off the west coast of Ireland)

Little new child
don't look at me
with your milky eyes
that tighten the muscles
of my womb so painfully.

I must harden myself against you.

Lie in your wooden crib
away from my arms
and from the breast
already aching
for your loss.

If you had been a girl
I could have held you longer.

But your brothers are calling you
from the pounding waves.
It was for the raging appetite
of the sea that I raised them.

New boy, don't search my face
for unconditional love;
we have to live
on this hard island
as best we can.

I will feed you, clothe you,
throw turf on the fire
to keep you warm,
but spare me
the ultimate penalty
of motherhood.

Your dangerous journey
away from me
as I lay alone
under the oilskins
that hang from the roof,
was pain enough.
I have no strength
for further partings.

Framed in this narrow window
the famished sea meets the sky
and gulls swirl upwards from it
like scorched paper from a bonfire.

Cottage at High Riley

I step backwards
on the dirt road
into your past
to see the house
where you were born,
on an October evening
such as this
when the trees are whipped
to a wild dance
by the moorland wind.

It stands in your landscape
of walled-in fields,
where the black cows lie,
above the grey town
whose people are as kind
as the weather is harsh.

A grey house
of sky coloured stone
and a stone roof,
the colour of tawny grass
that bends in the rain
with the nettles
at the roadside.

It is for sale.
Whoever buys it
may catch your first cry
from the old walls.
A sound I never heard,
who was a child
far away and in
a different place.

GWEN STANLEY

Dawn Chorus

I woke at dawn,
a swarm of thoughts
stinging tasks I had
awaiting me.

Then, calm, unhurried,
a cuckoo called out clear,
and all my day seemed
glad.

ANDREW STICKLAND

A Leaving Present

Here is something
to remember us by,
a delicate slice of Autumn
made rusty with leaves
and shrouded in copper
from a cold sunset.

And there is rain here,
brought on a grey wind
by pregnant clouds.
Take it, paint with it
the parched lips
of your new home

and you will find
soft memories budding
on awkward trees,
blossoming against the heat.
And when you return,
bring for us instead

a fiery young sun
in a clear blue sky,
a sudden brief shower,
warm and sweet,
and a handful of Spring
to scatter on the wind.

Evensong

Evening departs.
In the silence of the village
The old man's flute
Sings a requiem for the sun,
Notes dancing with housemartins
over silhouetted trees.

ELIZABETH ST JACQUES

A Star Shines On

> *in memory of Tom Cybolsky:*
> *The Renfrew Millionaires*
> *and Iroquois Falls Abitibi Eskimos*

Inside the frosty hockey rink
ice cracked and sprayed beneath his blades
steam burst from somewhere deep inside
to drive the puck into the net
again   again   again.

He never fooled himself;
it was the roaring crowd that scored
each and every time;
ice, rubber puck and stick
were instruments of love
that made him what he was —
a smalltown hockey star.

So many years ago . . .

Ninety when
his legs confined between white sheets
inside a hospital
he wandered back from time to time
to skate inside a dream,
and when some young reporter
searched dusty files to breath life into long past times,
the old star shone like new blue ice;
he heard the cheering crowds again
and knew that he still scored.

MILDRED TREMBLAY

Breasts and Bellies

In those days
my breasts and belly
like a field perhaps
ploughed by the moon
I was nature's favourite
I teemed with cycles
I waxed and waned
I swarmed with life
      oh it was splendid

I cast off the egg
I held the egg
birth raged through me
I arched   I heaved   I panted
I screamed beautifully
my body was a river
down which the blind babes
turned and twisted
lost their way
found it again

it seems my belly
was always sore
or tender or cramped
I was swollen or stretched
or bloody or torn
      oh it was splendid

my nipples powerful
tough and brown
sweet milk leaking
shaped to the pull
    of sucking mouths

I was like a garden
tilled   dug   seeded
I blossomed
I was always blossoming

now it is over

I am quiet

RUTH WALDRAM

The Studio At Aix

We knew at once he was there,
Gone for a coffee perhaps.
The guide-book said he was dead,
But in this great cube of a room
With its huge north light,
That was nonsense.

He was about to start work.
There was a new canvas on the easel
And a fistful of clean brushes crammed into a jar.
Tubes of paint rioted over the bench
Bright as a broken garland,
And the wiped palette
Waited.

All was to hand for a still-life:
A couple of wine bottles dark and lustrous,
Pots jostling cheek by jowl on the long shelf,
A white cloth thrown across the familiar table,
And a gather of garden flowers
Aflame
In a blue vase.

And apples galore!
Made bold by the confirming light
They shone, rotund and self-contained,
Solid, unique and bright.

These were the elect,
Waiting for the transubstantiation into paint
Which even as they rot
Bestows eternal life.

It was time for us to go.
He hadn't come back,
But no matter,
The encounter is all.

As we left we took three small pebbles from the gravel path
As a memento.
Rubbed in the pocket
They sing
Of resurrection.

JANET WALKER

Darkening Walk

Speaking a silent language
lizards in dry grasses
hold themselves to the sun's hot moment
in a noon day catch of breath.
Bursting broom pods crackle,
exploding into summer joy.
Beyond the charcoal hills
and brittle bones of ling,
gorses flame in nutty essences,
almond furnaces of yellow fire.
The greeny woods fizzle with oak.

Laurel bushes flank
the tunnelled entrance to the wood,
a burrow of dream birth
full of summer hungers,
an elf lane humming with pulses.
A rambler rose flows close
to the cheek of a journeying soul
swinging on see-saw spines.
In the comforting gloom
elders seep through saps of ilex.
Eye lanterns upturn to the owl.

Dark cedars are in still communion
and from their travelling branches
glint darkly in unfathomable speech.

MAUREEN WELDON

El Alamein 1942

They came one by one
El Alamein — the khaki inferno
Of smoke oil and yellow tongues.

For every one that lived
Two comrades died.

Now a million ghosts move silently
Buried in the ever moving sand,
Or talk in old men's dreams.

DUANE WILLIAMS

Nobody Said Anything

There was just the television
between them
and his father finally spoke. "Look at this,"
he said. "Crazy bastards. Now they're
killin' off themselves,"
he said, pointing at a black man
on the late world news, a tire burning
around the man's neck, smoke
and fists rising black
against the blue indignant sky
the crowd punching and kicking that man
children too with old, empty faces
throwing rocks, African words
the flames putting a look
on that man's face that was shameful
just to see, like the look on their dog's face
when his father used to beat it
for shitting on the carpet
and "It's come to this.
God fuckin' save us. It's come to this,"
his father said, pushing
a button, replacing Soweto
with a finicky Persian in pearls
"Let's go for a walk," he said.
"Let's get outta here."

They walked barefoot
through the chemical fog of his father's lawn
television blue flickering the neighbours'
windows, the electronic Delphic images
delivering oracles by the second
and a cat cried, haunting
like a baby, his father said, his father
who hated cats all his life
because they climb, jealous, into cribs
and the stars had fallen
beneath a millennium of wishes
but not the night's glass eye
staring at them, that cold shameless eye
and nobody said anything
about all those years of silence
just added that night
to the others, though who
was counting anymore
they were following their shadows
past insomniac televisions
it seemed enough, a small thing
and soon enough, they'd reach the end
turn back, satellites drifting in the voiceless darkness
above all that
they called their lives

RAY WILSON

"Good fences make good neighbours"

A thirsty region of reluctant rain,
acres of scrub, gaunt trees and dried-up dams.
But the grass is hardy — somehow it has survived —
and the rains *will* come.
The house is almost finished
but the land must yet be fenced.
Seven paddocks — 240 timber posts —
and endless kilometres of wire.
Back-breaking, arm-wrenching, fly-swatting work,
boring and digging, stomping in posts,
wielding cumbersome chainsaw and drill,
temperamental — with minds of their own.
But posts are set, stretchers fixed,
holes drilled, wires threaded and tightened.
The deadlines are met.
Fine house, fine paddocks, fine fences.
And the distant, curious neighbour
waves and shouts his greetings.
Friendly? Yes. But never forget
"Good fences make good neighbours."

MARGARET WINTER

The Journey Back

To a fishing village
high on the cliff
and clinging to the face of it
the steep and narrow road
winding down to the slipway.

To the small hotel
with views
across the windswept bay.

To the log fire
where now I stood
near the warm polished wood
of the galleried staircase.

To memories —
of a wartime year
when snow settled briefly
on the sand
and it was April.

JOAN WOODCOCK

Hands

For A.W.W.

Once my volunteer hands pushed wheel-chairs,
Carried cups of tea
With two nice Nice biscuits (and the little joke)
On the flowered saucers, year-in, year-out
For the white-haired cheerful monotonous Disabled Club.

Once I could skate, dance-flying in weightless joy,
Swaying with you to the Ice Rink's canned music,
Your hands firm forever on mine:
My hands ("Pale hands I loved
Beside the Shalimar . . . " our song) — my hands?

My autumn-mottled Grandmotherly hands
Clutching my walking frame? Who on earth is *that?*
Startled, looking quizzically, amusedly, at —
At me, in the mirror?
The old woman in the fairy tale, quavering
"Lawks-a-mussy-me, can this be truly *I?*"

But there is still the same small child
Inside my head, chuckling, enjoying, with my playmate
Grandchildren, another toy:
Granny Joan's funny new chair.
Their clamorous hands
Racing to work the lever, raising me
Effortlessly, to stand upright.
So much laughter to be shared,
And so much sheer, unadulterated fun in the world.

RICHARD WOOLLATT

Roy Ellergodt

I remember winters in the late forties
like you wouldn't believe
& on the Endiang sub
      north from Hanna
the line runs through a cut
the snow'd drift that right full
drifts eleven or twelve feet high
packed in hard.

We'd be out there with a snow-plow
— there was another engine & crew behind us
so if we'd get stuck in there
they'd hook onta us & pull us back —
the fella in the snowplow'd give you
the signal by a rope
one was stop
      two was go ahead
three back up
& you'd back away from this cut
throw the reverse lever down
open the throttle & go into this
as hard as you could
& then right away
      just before it'd stop
you'd grasp the reverse lever & pull it back
— usually you could —
but sometimes you got stuck in there
that snow was really packed hard

& I remember one time
we was burnin' Brazeau coal
but there was some briquettes in it
& I took a briquette
& the snowbank was right there
right agin the cab
& I made a mark on the snow
then we'd go back
take another run at it
we'd only go about two feet
but I'd mark where we stopped
& we'd do that hour after hour
sometimes fifteen hours on the job
before finally we got those cuts cleared.

The Poets

Anne Ashworth lives in Blackpool (England). She is an editor and former college librarian. *The Girl Who Runs Backwards* (prose and poetry) is forthcoming from The Pentland Press.

Winona Baker lives in Nanaimo (British Columbia). She was the International winner of the Basho Haiku Contest in 1989. Winona's books and chapbooks include: *Clouds Empty Themselves: Island Haiku, Not So Scarlet a Woman: Light and Humorous Poems, Moss-hung Trees: Haiku of the West Coast, Beyond the Lighthouse,* and *Wild Strawberries.*

David Barnett lives in Pencader (Carmarthenshire, Wales) in a remote Welsh farmhouse on the edge of the moorland. He was educated at Oxford University and he has travelled widely. David's publications are *The Mask of Siam, Bent in Water, Fretwork,* and *All The Year Round.*

Elinor Benedict: See page 119.

Paul Berry lives with his wife, Tina, and sons Daniel and Simon in King's Lynn (Norfolk, England) where he works in the National Health Service. He founded and co-ordinates Centre Poets and has edited *Poets' England: Norfolk.* Paul's five poetry publications are *The Cries of Ashes, Legacies, Earth Musk and Country Dark, A Bequest of Fire, Homages* and *Holiday Snaps.* He is also the author of *Airfield Heyday,* a social history of life on and around England's wartime airfields.

Mike Boland lives in Harrow Weald (Middlesex, England) where he works for the British government. He was born in 1950 in Kingston-on-Thames. In 1991 he organized the Poetry Workshop of the Society of Civil Service Authors. He also edits *The Arcadian,* a bi-annual poetry magazine. Mike won the Patricia Chowen Sonnet Competition (1991). His book is *The Midnight Circus* and he is one of four contributors to *The Trout...Minus One.*

Brian Burke lives in Vancouver (British Columbia). A graduate of the writing programs at York University and the University of British Columbia, he has taught English literature and creative writing at various colleges and universities. Brian's short fiction appears in *Stag Line: Stories by Men,* from Coteau Books.

Mavis Carter lives in Cirencester (Gloucestershire, England). She performs her poetry at festivals around the country as part of Grandmothers' Footsteps. As a singer she performed with The Cotswold Folk. Currently, Mavis is co-editing a new *Book of Blessings for England and Wales* for the Catholic Hierarchy. Her publications include *Seasonal Change* and *Turning Up the Volume.*

R.L. Cook lives in Kinross (Scotland). He is the author of seven poetry collections: *Hebrides Overture and Other Poems, Within the Tavern Caught, Sometimes a Word, Time with a Drooping Hand, The Daylight Lingers, World Elsewhere,* and *Voices from Ithaca.*

Barbara Crupi lives in Frating (Essex, England). She was born in 1943 in Suffolk. For over twenty years she was a partner with her husband on a family farm and she still maintains an extensive kitchen garden. Barbara's poetry collections are *Shadow Chasing* and *The Well Pool.*

Marguerite Dolsen lives in Burnaby (British Columbia). Her prairie pieces appear in *Saskatchewan History & Folklore Magazine,* a journal mainly dealing with pioneer history.

Gerald England was born in 1946 at Ackworth near Pontefract, the son of a Yorkshire miner, and now lives in Gee Cross, at the edge of the Pennines. Educated at Strathclyde University and Sheffield Polytechnic, he has worked as an industrial chemist in the confectionery trade and a financial advisor. He and his wife Christine have two sons, Strontian and Craig. Ten collections of his poems have been published: *Poetic Sequence for five voices; Mousings; The Wine the Women and the Song; For Her Volume One; Meetings; At the Moor's Edge; The Rainbow and Other Poems; Daddycation; Futures* (with Christine England); *Stealing Kisses;* and *Four Square Replay.* He has also written an account of 20 years of small press publishing, entitled *Editor's Dilemma,* drawing on his experience as editor of *Headland* and *New Hope International.* He enjoys motoring, islands and computing.

Ian Enters lives in Stocksbridge (South Yorkshire, England) where he serves as Curriculum Adviser for English for the Sheffield Education Authority. He was born in London in 1947 and was educated at Trinity College, Oxford. Ian is married and has four children. His volumes of poetry are *Outside This Communion, Calendar of the Greeks,* and *Build and Break;* his two novels are *Shadow* and *Up to Scratch.*

Katherine L. Gordon lives in Eramosa Township near Guelph (Ontario). She edits *The Eramosa Anthology* and has contributed to international anthologies. Her work is inspired largely by the natural world and its vital connection to the human condition.

David A. Groulx lives in Thunder Bay (Ontario) where he attends Lakehead University. He is an Ojibwa. In 1995 he won the Munro Family Poetry Prize.

Richard M. Grove lives in Toronto (Ontario) where he edits *SEEDS,* a poetry review which exists both on paper and on the World Wide Web (http://www.pathcom.com/~writers). Tai, as he is known to friends, exhibits his poetry in acrylic on paper paintings and in audio sculptures. His first book is *Beyond Fear & Anger.*

Alistair Halden lives in Fearnan (Perthshire, Scotland) in a house beside Loch Tay. Born in 1929, he is a retired English teacher who has just finished a whodunnit called *Death at the Leck*. He has won several literary awards and prizes, among them: the Greenwich Festival (1984) and the Scottish International Open Poetry Competition (The MacDiarmid Trophy). Alistair's poetry chapbook is *To Travel Hopefully*. He is married to Joyce and they have three children and four grandchildren.

Margaret B. Hammer lives in Dartmouth (Nova Scotia). She was a finalist in the League of Canadian Poets' National Poetry Contest (1990). Her book is *Dim Time and History on a Garrison Clock*.

F. R. Harris lives in Hove (Sussex, England). He is a retired supermarket manager and is married, with four grown children. His publications include *Late Harvest* (poems and prose on cassette), *One Man's Tread* (poetry and prose), *Bridge Over Today* (poetry), and *Bridge Over Yesterday* (local history). He is in the process of writing a novel.

David Hillen lives in Hamilton (Ontario) with his wife, Janet. They have four children: Heather, Andrew, Amanda, and Stephen. He has been a classroom teacher for thirty years and is currently head of a secondary school English department. He edited *Indirections*, the journal of the English Teachers of Ontario, and has received several awards, including the OSSTF Henry Hunter Memorial Fellowship and an Arts Council grant. David is a contributor to *A Cliff Runs Through It*, Hamilton's sesquicentennial anthology.

Mary Hodgson lives in Eastham (Merseyside, England). She was born in Ipswich and moved to the Wirral when she married. She has three children. Her poetry has been broadcast on BBC Northwest and Radio Merseyside. Mary's publications are *Waiting to Cross*, *New World*, and *Summer World*. The latter two chronicle travel in the U.S.

Peter Howard lives in Milton (Cambridgeshire, England). He works as a telecommunications systems and design consultant in Cambridge. Born in Nottingham in 1957, Peter read physics and philosophy at Hertford College, Oxford. He writes a column on Internet poetry for *Poetry Review*. His chapbook collection is *Low Probability of Racoons*.

Winifred N. Hulbert lives in Hamiota (Manitoba) where she and her husband are retired farmers. She has read her poetry on both radio and TV. Winifred's books are *Echoes*, *Down My Road*, and *Moth and Candle*.

Sheila Hyland lives in Toronto (Ontario) where she leads workshops and runs the Canadian Poetry Association's Metro Toronto Chapter. She is originally from England and has read her poetry on both sides of the Atlantic. She is the editor of *Strong Winds*, an anthology of poetry by CPA members. Among Sheila's poetry collections are *On Grenadier Pond*, *Love Lines*, *A Given Line*, and *Misty Willows*.

Laura H. Kennedy lives in Stratford (Connecticut) where she works as a Price Waterhouse LLP Marketing Specialist. She is a member of the International Women Writer's Guild and the Connecticut Poetry Society. Laura has recorded a collection of poems from *Still Filled with Light,* a chapbook, at the Teachers and Writers Collaborative, New York. The program aired on October 26, 1995.

Mary Kratt lives in Charlotte (North Carolina), where she teaches part-time at the University of North Carolina. She has eleven published books of poetry, history, and biography, the most recent of which is *On the Steep Side*. Her chapbook *The Only Thing I Fear is a Cow and a Drunken Man* won the Oscar Arnold Young Award. Mary is also twice winner of the Blumenthal Writers and Readers Series, 1994 winner of the Fortner Writer-in-Community Award, and 1996 winner of a North Carolina Arts Council fellowship to the MacDowell Colony in New Hampshire.

Cecil Justin Lam lives in Toronto (Ontario) where he edits *Chastity and Holiness* and *Polyglot Army*. He is the author of several chapbooks, including *The Orange Rainbow, the Purple Rainbow*.

John B. Lee lives in Brantford (Ontario). He was born in 1951 and was raised on a farm. The most honoured writer of his generation, he is the only poet to win the Milton Acorn Memorial People's Poetry Award twice (1993 & 1995). He also is a winner of the Tilden Canadian Literary Award for Poetry (CBC Radio/Saturday Night) and several other prizes. He is the editor of *That Sign of Perfection,* a collection of hockey poems and stories. His twenty-one books and chapbooks (mostly poetry) are: *Poems Only a Dog Could Love, Love Among the Tombstones, To Kill a White Dog, Fossils of the Twentieth Century, Broken Glass, Hired Hands, Small Worlds, The Day Jane Fonda Came to Guelph, Rediscovered Sheep, The Bad Philosophy of Good Cows, The Pig Dance Dreams, The Hockey Player Sonnets, When Shaving Seems Like Suicide, Variations on Herb, The Art of Walking Backwards, All The Cats Are Gone, What's in a name?, These Are the Days of Dogs and Horses, Head Heart Hands Health: A History of 4-H in Ontario, The Beatles Landed Laughing in New York,* and *Tongues of the Children*.

Anne Lewis-Smith lives in Newport (Dyfed, Wales). Over fifty years, she has edited many magazines, including *Envoi,* and served as managing director of *Envoi Poets Publications*. (Over thirty of the poets collected in this volume have had books or chapbooks with Envoi Poets Publications.) She has now retired from editing others' work to concentrate on her own. Her eighth poetry book has just been published; the ninth will consist entirely of love poems. Anne is a balloonist with nearly thirty years' experience, a grandmother, an inveterate scribbler, and a lover of islands.

Noah Leznoff lives in Markham (Ontario) with his wife and two daughters. His most recent book of poetry is *Why We Go To Zoos*.

Michael Londry is a graduate student in English literature at the University of Alberta (Edmonton). His poems have been broadcast on CBC Radio and he has twice been awarded the James Patrick Folinsbee Prize for Poetry. A selection of his work appears in *Breathing Fire: Canada's New Poets*.

Hugh MacDonald lives near Montague (Prince Edward Island) along the south bank of the Montague River. He is married to Sandra and they have a well blended family of five sons and a daughter. Hugh has been an actor as well as a director of school and community productions. He is the author of a children's book, *Chung Lee Loves Lobsters,* and a volume of poetry, *Looking For Mother,* that celebrates his mother and her struggle with Alzheimer Disease.

Tanis MacDonald divides her time between Winnipeg (Manitoba) and Toronto (Ontario), and between teaching and writing. She is the author of the forthcoming *Breathing November* and of *This Speaking Plant*, the winner of the 1996 Acorn-Rukeyser Chapbook Award.

Colin Mackay lives in Edinburgh (Scotland) where he works as a nightwatchman. He is the author of three novels: *The Song of the Forest, The Sound of the Sea,* and *House of Lies*. His volume of poetry is *Red Ice*. A second poetry collection, dealing with the Bosnian war, should appear next year.

John Marks lives in Manchester (England) with his Irish wife and five children. He is a tutor at The Open University. He is also a cricket fan. John's collections are *Soundbites* and *Lifting the Veil*.

Joy Martin lives in the small seaside town of Swanage (Dorset, England). She has won several poetry prizes. For the past eight years, Joy has organized the Swanage Arts Festival International Literary Competition, inaugurated ten years ago by her late husband, Lewis Hosegood.

Catherine McCausland lives in Tors Cove (Newfoundland). With a husband at sea and a family to raise, Catherine's daily experiences influence her work as a writer and textile artist.

Jane McCreery is co-host and co-producer of "Prosody" on WYEP in Pittsburgh, Western Pennsylvania's only weekly radio program devoted to contemporary poetry. She is best known for collaborations combining her poetry with work by artists from other genres, including painting, sculpture, photography and modern dance. She recently studied at the University of Iowa with Timothy Liu.

Derrick McIntosh lives in Palmerston, a farming region in midwestern Ontario, where he was born in 1979. He is a student at Norwell District Secondary School. Derrick has been a prize winner in the Dorothy Shoemaker Literary Competition as well as the Wellington County Poetry Contest.

Elise McKay lives in Edinburgh (Scotland). She is a widow with a son, a daughter, and five grandchildren. Elise trained as a nurse (Edinburgh Royal Infirmary) and as a teacher (Jordanhill College) and came to poetry late in life. She has won several poetry prizes, among them the Fulham and Hammersmith Festival of poetry. Her books are *Unravelling Knots* and *Floating Lanterns*.

Hilary Mellon lives in Norwich (Norfolk, England) where she was born in 1949. She teaches adult education classes in creative writing and twentieth-century poetry. Hilary's poetry is widely anthologized. Her books and chapbooks are *Night With An Old Raincoat, Alarmed by Dawn, Disturbing the Night, Fire Raiser,* and *Spaces Inbetween*.

Chad Norman lives in Burnaby (British Columbia) where he and his partner, Catherine Owen, run the Royal City Poetry Centre Reading Series. Chad was born in Armstrong (B.C.) in 1959. His first 'real' book, *The Breath of One,* will be published later this year.

Mary Nugent lives in Whitstable (Kent, England). She only started to write after marriage. Her chapbook is *The Game*.

Margaret Pain lives in Woking (Surrey, England), where she was born. Since 1978 she had been a co-editor of *Weyfarers* and for many years she served as assistant editor of *Envoi*. She was Deputy Chairman or Chairman of the Surrey Poetry Centre and Wey Poets for many years. Her poetry has won several prizes, including the New Poetry Competition and the Surrey Poetry Centre Open Competition. Margaret has written four chapbook collections: *Walking to Eleusis, No Dark Legend, A Fox in the Garden,* and *Shadow Swordsman*.

Peggy Poole lives in West Kirby (Merseyside, England) by the River Dee. She recently retired from being Poetry Consultant to the BBC North's "Write Now". As an editor, she has seen three anthologies into print: *Windfalls, Poet's England 17: Cumbria,* and *Marigolds Grow Wild on Platforms*. Peggy is the author of several children's books and an adult novella. Her poetry publications are *Never a Put-up Job, Cherry Stones and other poems, No Wilderness in them, Midnight Walk, Hesitations, Trusting the Rainbow, Bruised,* and *Rich Pickings*.

Barbara Rennie lives in Stoke Fleming (South Devon, England). She is the only writer to have won the Julia Cairns Award of the Society of Women Writers and Journalists three times (1987, 1988, & 1990), Barbara's publications are *The Sky Wandered By, As If —,* and *The Fifty-minute Hour*.

Louise Rogers lives in Ruislip (Middlesex, England), near the woodlands of which she writes. She seeks poetry in all facets of art, music, and the natural world. She is the proud mother of two grown sons, and the author of *Such Stars I Counted Mine*.

Carol Rose: See page 118.

K.V. Skene is a Canadian poet living in Langton Matravers (Dorset, England). Skene is the author of two chapbooks, *Pack Rat* and *The Uncertainty Factor/As A Rock,* as well as a full-size collection, *fire water.*

Deirdre Armes Smith has lived in Worsley (Greater Manchester, England) all her life. She has four children, eleven grandchildren, and one great-grandchild and still finds time to read her poetry regularly on Radio Merseyside and Radio Manchester. Deirdre is the author of seven books: *Cycles of the Moon, Church Bells on a Wet Sunday, Winter Tennis Courts, The Real Thing, With Untold Care, Mother of Wales, Drawn by the Moon,* and *Invisible Lady.*

John Souster lives in Wallingford (England). He was born in Northampton in 1912 but grew up in New Zealand. He is a retired horticulturist and a World War II vet. John's poetry collection is *Looking Before and After.*

Gwen Stanley lives in Formby (Merseyside, England) where she is an English lecturer. She was born in Yorkshire in 1934. Gwen reads her poetry on local radio and her collection is *Stabling The Thoroughbred.*

Andrew Stickland is studying creative writing at the University of Jyväskylä, Finland. His permanent residence is in Peterborough (Cambridgeshire, England). He was born in Forres (Scotland) in 1966, but spent much of his life in Lincolnshire. Andrew studied law at University College, London. He has three collections: *Broken Bottles, The Opposite Page,* and *Mathematical Love.*

Elizabeth St Jacques lives in Sault Ste-Marie (Ontario). A published writer for 30 years, her work has been published in ten countries. She is the author of eight books, including *Around the Tree of Light,* the first collection of original English-language sijo poetry published in North America. Her 1995 haiku collection, *A Dance of Light,* earned the Merit Book Award Winner (Haiku Society of America), a 1995 Albatross Award (Romania) & was among *Small Press Review's* "November Picks", 1995. She is associate editor of *Sijo West,* poetry editor of *Canadian Writer's Journal,* and contributing editor of *Small Press Review.*

Mildred Tremblay lives in Nanaimo (British Columbia). She has a collection of short stories from Oolichan Press. She is the winner of the 1996 Poet of the Year competition (*Arc* magazine) and placed second in the League of Canadian Poets' annual competition.

Ruth Waldram lives in Cambridge (England). Born in 1906, she began writing poetry during the long, dark blackout evenings of World War II, when she was evacuated with three small children. She did not write seriously again until the 1980s, when old age once more gave her mind time to roam. Her poetry collection is *Another Spring.*

Janet Walker lives in Waddington (Lincolnshire, England) and is a retired school teacher. She was born in 1941 and is a poet, musician, and mystic as well as being, on a more practical level, a wife, mother, and granny. Janet's poetry book is *Translucent Silks*.

Maureen Weldon lives in Upton-by-Chester (Cheshire, England). An Irishwoman and a former dancer with the Irish Theatre Ballet Company, her poetry is heard on Radio Merseyside. Maureen has one chapbook and three books of poetry to her credit: *Leap, No Pawns In This Play,* and *Of Crossed Wires.*

Duane Williams lives in Hamilton (Ontario). He is the author of the chapbook, *Taste The Silence.* Duane's short stories have appeared in *Queeries* and *Queer View Mirror* among other publications.

Jim C. Wilson lives in Edinburgh (Scotland) with his wife, Mik. He was born in 1948 and studied English at Edinburgh University. He was writing fellow for Stirling District from 1989-1991. Jim won The MacDiarmid Trophy in the 1997 Scottish International Open Poetry Competition. His poetry collections are *The Loutra Hotel* and *Cellos in Hell.*

Ray Wilson was born in Co. Durham (England); on retirement he moved to Glenore Grove (Queensland, Australia), where he enjoys singing, amateur theatricals, chess, and gardening. Two of his children have also moved to Australia, and the other two are on the way. Ray's teaching experience includes Lecturer in English at Westminster College of Education, Oxford, and a stint in Malaya with the Royal Army Educational Corps. His poetry collection is *An Apple for Alex.*

Margaret Winter lived in Hunmanby (North Yorkshire, England). She was born in 1921 and was brought up in Cottingham (East Yorkshire). Margaret served in World War II in the W.R.N.S. In 1952 she and her husband, John, emigrated to Canada and lived there twenty-eight years, chiefly in Oakville (Ontario) They returned to England in 1980. Her chapbook of poems is called *Legacy.*

Joan Woodcock lives in Malmesbury (Wiltshire, England). Although she could not fulfil her hopes of university education, she considers herself lucky to have been able to begin a career on Fleet Street, in 1927, at the age of 19. She is still writing at age 89. Her most recent poetry collections are *Borrowing from Time* and *Stabbed Awake.*

Richard Woollatt lives in Burlington (Ontario) with his wife Frances. He was born during the Depression (1932) and raised in Alberta. He is a freelance writer and photographer and a retired teacher. Along with the celebrated People's Poet Raymond Souster, Richard edited four major anthologies: *Generation Now, Sights and Sounds, These loved, these hated lands,* and *Poems of a Snow-Eyed Country.* He also edited *Flight of the Roller Coaster,* a collection of Souster's verse for younger readers. His own poetry books are *Eastbound From Alberta and Border Crossings.* He is a contributor to *Ingots,* Hamilton's Sesquicentennial Anthology.

Acknowledgements

"Window" and "The Place of Wolves" by Mavis Carter are from her book *Turning up the Volume*, Envoi Poets Publications, 1994. "Chiselling the Dark" was first published in *Patchwork* magazine.

"High-Rise Mondrian" by Margaret B. Hammer is from her book *Dim Time and History on a Garrison Clock*, Roseway Publishing, 1993.

"We Had Our Targets" by F.R. Harris is from his book *Bridge Over Today*, Envoi Poets Publications, 1989.

"Saybrook Point, Connecticut" by Mary Hodgson is from *New World*, Envoi Poets Publications, 1990.

"Manitoba Farmers" by Winifred N. Hulbert is from her book *Down My Road*, 1979.

"Summer Daze" by Sheila Hyland is from her book *Love Lines*, Sheis Press, 1994.

"Leaving Ash Creek" by Laura H. Kennedy was first published in *Hermes' Crossing* magazine.

"Morning Report" by Cecil Justin Lam is from his book *The Orange Rainbow, The Purple Rainbow*, The Plowman, 1994.

"The Coal Miners" by John B. Lee was first published in *The Amethyst Review*. "The Winter of 96" was first published in *Outreach* newspaper.

"the wind is blowing me away!" and "In Moonlight After Rain" by Noah Leznoff are from his book *Why We Go To Zoos*, Insomniac Press, 1997.

"Behind the Red Brick House" by Hugh MacDonald was frist published in *That Sign of Perfection*, Black Moss Press, 1995.

"Service with a Smile" by Tanis MacDonald is from *This Speaking Plant*, Unfinished Monument Press, 1997, the winner of the Acorn-Rukeyser Chapbook Contest.

"Bosnia" by John Marks is from his book *Lifting the Veil*, New Hope International, 1997.

"Marbled Moon" by Hilary Mellon was first published in *And God Created Woman* (anthology).

"Rievaulx Abbey" by Mary Nugent is from her book *The Game*, Envoi Poets Publications.

"Dawn Watch" by Margaret Pain is from her book *No Dark Legend*, Hub Publications, 1977.

"Needlewoman" by Peggy Poole is from her book *Midnight Walk and Other Poems*, Envoi Poets Publications, 1986.

"Entering Cold Woodlands" by Louise Rogers was first published in *Green Leaf and Blue Water*.

"pillar of salt" and "they talk theology instead" by Carol Rose are from her book *Behind the Blue Gate*, Beach Holme Publishers, 1997.

"Learning Death" by K.V. Skene was first published in *The Interpreter's House*, issue 3.

"To John Clare" by John Souster was first published in *Openings 2*.

"The Journey Back" by Margaret Winter is from her book *Legacy*, Envoi Poets Publications.

"Hands" by Joan Woodcock is from her book *Borrowing From Time*, Envoi Poets Publications.

Contest judge, Fred Cogswell

Fred Cogswell is the author of a great many poetry books. These include *The Stunted Strong, Descent from Eden, Lost Dimension, In Praise of Chastity, The House Without a Door, Light Bird of Life, A Long Apprenticeship, Pearls, Selected Poems, Meditations: 50 Sestinas, When the Right Light Shines, In Praise of Old Music, In My Own Growing,* and *As I See It.* Dr. Cogswell is also the translator and editor of *One Hundred Poems of Modern Quebec, A Second Hundred Poems of Modern Quebec, The Poetry of Modern Quebec,* and *Unfinished Dreams: Contemporary Poetry of Acadia.*

His anthologies of English-language literature include *The Atlantic Anthology* (two volumes), *The Arts in New Brunswick,* and *The Enchanted Land.* He also edited a special Canadian issue of *Outposts,* the first serious introduction of Canadian poetry to British readers.

For many years he edited *The Fiddlehead*, a leading Canadian literary magazine. He also founded Fiddlehead Poetry Books (now called Goose Lane Editions) and published over one hundred poetry collections before he retired.

Dr. Cogswell has been appointed a Member of the Order of Canada. He has also been awarded the Gold Medal of the Philippines Republic for his work as both a poet and magazine editor. Over the years, Dr. Cogswell has received honours from several universities for his contribution to Canadian letters. These institutions include St. Francis Xavier University, King's College, and Mount Allison University.

We are greatly honoured to have had Fred Cogswell serve as judge.

Prizewinner
Carol Rose

My poems are inspired by women's efforts to make meaning of their lives in a culture that has either silenced or denied their experience. Frequently my poems wrestle with "master stories" found in biblical text. First I look at the traditional ways in which women have been portrayed in that narrative. Then I try to bring to light neglected elements in the tales, sometimes offering creative retellings. I shift the emphasis of the stories, moving women from the periphery to the very centre of their own stories. In that sense, my work challenges the stereotypes in sacred text.

I also raise questions about the tangle of issues and emotions that bind the Israeli and the Palestinian peoples, and about the ways in which the media choose to portray their struggles toward a whole and just peace. Jerusalem, both as metaphor and as landscape, figures heavily in my imagery. I believe that this ancient/modern site holds a promise of redemption for those who, like me, engage in the process of recreating the world through words.

> Carol Rose, a writer, teacher, and counsellor, lives in Winnipeg (Manitoba, Canada) with her husband and daughter. She is the mother of five children. Carol has won awards and honours in several contests, including second prize at the 1994 Stephen Leacock International Poetry Awards. She has been nominated for the 1997 John Hirsch Award for most promising Manitoba writer. Carol has contributed poems and articles to numerous Jewish and feminist anthologies. Currently she is co-editing (with Joan Turner) an anthology titled *Spider Women: A Tapestry of Creativity and Healing.* Her first book, *Behind the Blue Gate,* appeared this year.

Prizewinner Elinor Benedict

For me, poetry brings memory and imagination together to create a new experience that explores and discovers, reconciles and transmits. Yes, transmits. I do not wish to shut the reader out. I want poetry to wrestle with meaning, or at least to illuminate that tangled path. I value clarity; mystery for mystery's sake does not satisfy me, nor does language for language's sake. I do not worship poetry. In my credo, poetry is not a substitute for faith, love, and grace, but rather a means to examine them. And since there is enough poison in the world, I would not willingly create flowers of evil to gain attention. Making beauty out of ugliness is a feat of creation I aspire to only if the ugliness is not my own creation. The bugaboo of sentimentality, of course, may seem to lurk in such a goal. The only antidote to this danger is excellence of art and craft. Imagery and story are my chief tools. No, I do not always meet my own criteria for poetry. The elements of humour, irony, and play must often compensate for the lack of perfection both in my humanity and in my art and craft.

> Elinor Benedict, a native of Tennessee and graduate of Duke University, earned an MA in English from Wright State University, Ohio, and an MFA in Writing from Vermont College. She has won several awards, including the Mademoiselle Fiction Prize and an Editor's Grant, as founding editor of *Passages North* literary magazine, from the Coordinating Council of Literary Magazines (now CLMP). She lives in the Upper Peninsula of Michigan. She has published three chapbooks with a China theme, *A Bridge to China*, *The Green Heart*, and *Chinavision*, all part of a larger collection based on family relationships and trips to China.

About Carl Sandburg

Carl Sandburg (1878–1967) worked at many jobs — day laborer, hobo, dishwasher, soldier, farm hand, and newspaper reporter — before publishing his first volume of poetry at the age of almost forty years. His poetry titles include *Chicago Poems, Cornhuskers, Smoke and Steel, Slabs of the Sunburnt West, Good Morning, America, The People, Yes, Honey and Salt,* and *Billy Sunday and Other Poems.* Sandburg twice won the Pulitzer Prize for poetry. He won a third Pulitzer for his history of Abraham Lincoln's Civil War years. All told, over thirty books of poetry, fiction, non-fiction, and children's literature bear his name.

In addition to his work for daily newspapers in Chicago, Sandburg also wrote for the *International Socialist Review* and *The Masses*. He founded what Selden Rodman called Proletarian Poetry (now better known as Populist Poetry) and inspired many of the poets who came onto the American scene during the 1930s, such as Muriel Rukeyser, Kenneth Fearing, and the Benét brothers.

A realist who always had a broad romantic streak, Sandburg never surrendered his faith in the basic goodness of the People. His poetry was therefore noted for its rock-hard strength as well as its drifting-fog tenderness. At the time of his death he was America's favorite poet.

About Dorothy Livesay

Dorothy Livesay (1909–1996) had a remarkable seventy-year literary career. Livesay was a leading People's Poet, literary editor, magazine publisher, mentor, feminist, and social justice activist. She was one of the first poets in Canada to write about Marxism, the lives of working people, and women's sexuality. She also took on the taboo subject of aging as she herself grew older. In fact, there was no subject Livesay was afraid to tackle. While she was still an undergraduate at the University of Toronto, Livesay took on campus sexism and the academic establishment. And while active in the League of Canadian Poets she took on professional and academic elitism. She was a supporter of gay and lesbian rights when almost no one else was.

With her third and fourth books — *Day and Night* (1944) and *Poems for People* (1947), both Governor General's Award winners — she set the tone for People's Poetry in Canada. Indeed, much of the poetry written during the 1950s, '60s, and '70s was inspired by her example. Livesay's influence can be seen in the work of Margaret Atwood, Milton Acorn, Al Purdy, and Rhea Tregebov. Her selected poems, *The Self-Completing Tree,* is a definitive work. Her strong words and stronger deeds are missed by all who love Canadian poetry.

Other Books by Unfinished Monument/Mekler & Deahl

Poetry

Milton Acorn, **To Hear the Faint Bells:**
   haiku, senryu and short poems from Canada's national poet
James Deahl (editor): **Mix Six**
James Deahl (editor): **The Northern Red Oak:**
   poems for and about Milton Acorn
Simon Frank, **Imaginary Poems**
LeRoy Gorman (editor), **Gathering Light:** The Herb Barrett Award
Albert W.J. Harper. **Poems of Reflection**
I.B. Iskov, **black and white**
Mohammad Khan, **The Unmuffled Voices of El Dorado**
Audrey Duncan Major, **Light & Lively Poems, Book II**
Tanis MacDonald, **This Speaking Plant**
   (The Acorn-Rukeyser Award)
Judge Mazebedi, **Chicken Cries Out**
Ted Plantos (editor), **Not to Rest in Silence:**
   A celebration of people's poetry
Anna Plesums, **Intrinsic Revelations**
Anna Plesums, **Love and Words**
Kay Redhead, **The Song of the Artichoke Lover**
Jeff Seffinga, **Bailey's Mill**
Jeff Seffinga (editor), **A Cliff Runs Through It**
Jeff Seffinga (editor), **Ingots**
Jeff Seffinga, **Tight Shorts:** haiku and other short poems
Adèle Kearns Thomas, **Behind the Scenes**

Non-fiction

Edda Maria Favretto-Post, **One Day She Will Fly:**
   A survivor's story of a traumatic brain injury
David Allen Greene, **The Script of Under the Watchful Eye**
Claire Ridker & Patricia Savage, **Railing Against the Rush of Years:**
   A personal journey through aging via art therapy
Elsa Thon, **I Wish It Were Fiction:** Memories 1939–1945

Mekler & Deahl also distributes the works of several literary presses, including Agenda Editions (England), Acumen Publications (England), Third Eye (Canada), and Owl's Head Press (Canada).